Deb & Sergio's REAL DEAL on GLOBAL WARMING

by Al Sonja Schmidt

THE "OTHER-SIDE" OF THE MAN-MADE GLOBAL WARMING ISSUE

AuthorHouse™
1663 Liberty Drive, Suite 200
Bloomington, IN 47403
www.authorhouse.com
Phone: 1-800-839-8640

This book is a work of fiction. People, places, events, and situations are the product of the author's imagination. Any resemblance to actual persons, living or dead, or historical events, is purely coincidental.

This book is a work of non-fiction. Unless otherwise noted, the author and the publisher make no explicit guarantees as to the accuracy of the information contained in this book and in some cases, names of people and places have been altered to protect their privacy.

Illustrations by Tanya Roberts and Cheri Graham.

© 2008 Al Sonja Schmidt. All Rights Reserved.

No part of this book may be reproduced, stored in a retrieval system, or transmitted by any means without the written permission of the author.

First published by AuthorHouse 3/31/2008

ISBN: 978-1-4343-2057-5 (sc)

Library of Congress Control Number: 2008900871

Printed in the United States of America
Bloomington, Indiana

This book is printed on acid-free paper..

> **TO ROB**
> **FOR YOUR NEVER-ENDING SUPPORT, STRENGTH AND LOVE.**
> **I COULDN'T HAVE DONE THIS WITHOUT YOU.**

ACKNOWLEDGMENTS

MANY SPECIAL THANKS TO: Cheri Graham for your "kid-feedback", for cataloging artwork and for many of the adorable illustrations; Jonathan and Darlene for your encouragement; Tim Ball and Paul Driessen for taking time out of your busy schedules to help me with this book; to the many specialists on this topic who have courageously spoken out to try to set the record straight. And a super big thanks to "Reeks" whose passionate belief that all weather events are caused by global warming motivated me to write this book.

FOREWORD

It's The Hysteria, Stupid!

My four children, none old enough to drive a Prius, are drowning in a sea of Global Warming propaganda. From the opening school bell, a hurricane of disinformation wreaks havoc on their innocent minds. And when they come home the happy-go-lucky cartoons of old are now replaced with climate change cautionary tales covered in the sheep's clothing of animation. *"Happy Feet"*? Not after they watched that movie!

The fun is being drained from the reservoir of youth. The levees of our kids' brains are virtually defenseless from the onslaught of alarmism. And if we don't do something soon, a tidal wave of disastrous political remedies will destroy the progress and ingenuity of mankind! Fear not, good parent, for the end is not nigh. In fact the skies are blue – if you just open your eyes.

Instead of playing the scare game, best friends Deb and Seby with the help of Al Sonja Schmidt, take a higher road and trade in cool, incontrovertible facts. I may be pushing forty, but *"The Real Deal on Global Warming"* was a valuable information resource for me. Of course, my children will also be required to read the book after each and every time they are forced in school to watch Al Gore's *"An Inconvenient Truth"*. So be a good global citizen and recycle this book -- by making sure every child in your life reads it! Their sanity may depend on it.

Andrew Breitbart

TABLE OF CONTENTS

INTRODUCTION

1 – PLANET EARTH -- TOO HOT, OR NOT?   1

    Don't Worry, Chill-ax!   2
    Warming and Cooling Is So Old News   4
    Warm Weather? ...Cool!   7

2 - THE REAL DEAL ON MAN-MADE GLOBAL WARMING   9

    Greenhouse Gases   10
    Humans Aren't the Boss of Earth   14
    Earth is Awesome!   15

3 - GREENHOUSE GASES AND EARTH   17

    Man vs. Volcanoes   18
    Vapor & Sunshine & Beasts, Oh My!   20

4 - INDUSTRY AND GLOBAL WARMING   24

   The Real Deal on Industry   25
   Industry, So Cool!   29
   If Industry is So Bad, Why Does the Rest of the World Want It?   36

5 - DON'T WORRY EARTH! WE'LL FIX YOU!   39

   Follow the Leader   40
   Carbon Up-sets   43
   CFL Bulbs & Whatnot   45

6 - WHY DOES IT SEEM SO REAL?!   50

   Boo!!   51
   "The Most Serious Issue of Our Time"!   55
   No Escape!   58
   Sticks and Stones   59

7 - WHO'S TELLING US THIS SCARY STUFF AND WHY?   63

   The Media   64
   Hollywood Wack-A-Do's   67
   Schools   69
   Politicians   70
   Billions of Reasons to Promote Global Warming!   71

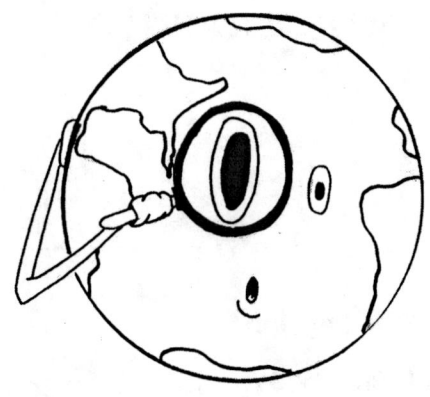

8 - X-TREMIE GREENIE MEANIES!!   74

    Down With People!   75
    Down With Freedom!   79
    Mean Green Environmental Machine!   81

9 - THE GREENIES WHO CRIED, WOLF!!   85

    Eco - Oopsies!   86

10 - WHAT ABOUT THE POLAR BEARS?!   89

    Bearly Honest   90
    Bearly Truthful   96
    Lots and Lots of Polar Bears!   98
    Still Worried?   99

11 - OKAY, SO HOW DO I TAKE CARE OF THE EARTH?   101

    Good Stewardship   102

12 - CHECK IT OUT!   104

    More Real Deal!   105

INTRODUCTION

Hi, I'm **Deb** and this is my best friend, **Seby**.

If you're freaking out about global warming like Seby, this book is for you.

It's fun, sometimes silly, and isn't written in long chapters with giant words or scientific explanations, just brief key points! Short and sweet! Simple and easy! When you're done, if you want more information on global warming, you can check out some of our favorite websites, movies and other books on this hot topic. They're all listed in the last chapter!

So, if you're ready to read, let's go! But you've got to do one thing first.

BECAUSE, LUCKILY...

THE REAL DEAL IS -- All this scary global warming stuff is probably not as bad as you think.

CHAPTER 1

PLANET EARTH -- TOO HOT, OR NOT?

DON'T WORRY, CHILL-AX!

WE HEAR...

Earth is getting hot!

It's being destroyed!

Soon, we can't hang out on it anymore!

Ahhhhhhh!!!!!!

There are many different opinions about what is going on with earth's current temperature trend, what's causing it, and what it means to earth's future. But there is one thing we can all agree on...

EARTH GETS WARMER!!

BUT CHILL-AX, it's only a phase. You can relate to that, right? Remember when you thought butterfly clips were going to stay in style forever?

Just like you, earth goes through phases. It gets cooler …then warmer, then cooler, then warmer, then … Well, you get the picture. Temperature change is one of many natural occurrences on earth. It's what earth does!

But warming trends also depend on what period of time you're talking about. True, earth has gotten warmer in the past 100-150 years, but only by A LITTE BIT! On the other hand since 1998 the global temperature has actually gone down!

GLOBAL WARMING - The progressive gradual rise of the earth's surface temperature.

THE REAL DEAL IS -- Earth goes through changes just like you and me. Its temperature has warmed and cooled for millions of years and it will continue, because that's what earth does!

WARMING AND COOLING IS SO, OLD NEWS!

Earth's warming and cooling is simply not new news. These changes are as old as earth itself. A long time ago it went into a cold phase called…...

LITTLE ICE AGE

THE REAL DEAL IS Little Ice Age was a period when the winters were cold in Northern Europe and North America.

ICE AGE - Intervals during which glaciers get larger and smaller. Over 60 glacial advances and retreats have occurred during the last 2 million years. Even now some glaciers are growing while others are shrinking.

But before the Little Ice Age earth went through a very different phase. It was a warming phase called...

MEDIEVAL WARM PERIOD

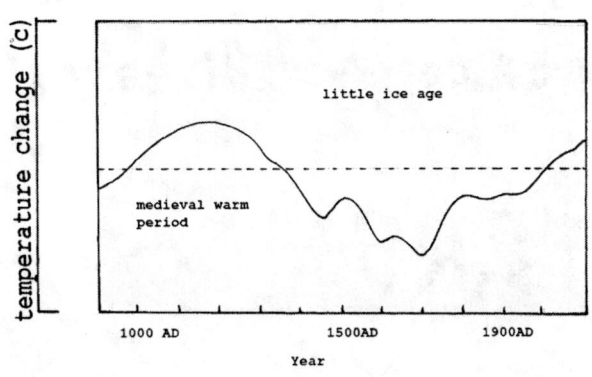

By the way, the Medieval Warm Period was much warmer than it is today!

So, if the earth's climate has been hotter before (and cooler before), why is the idea of a new warming phase reported like brand new, first-time-ever, earth-shattering news?

Well, **THE REAL DEAL IS**, in the late 1800's newspapers and magazines warned their readers about the,

Looming danger of a new ice age!!

Then in the late 1920's when the earth's surface warmed (only by less than half a degree) newspapers and magazines warned their readers about the,

Looming danger as the earth grows warmer!!

Today, reporters are totally kicking it up a notch. Now they're warning that a rise in global warming will bring about horrifying consequences.

Massive floods!

Terrible storms!

Out of control diseases!

And...

MONSTERS!

Okay, maybe the whole monster thing is an exaggeration. But according to many respected scientists, researchers, and professors from all around the world, so are those scary global disaster predictions! **THE REAL DEAL IS**, they all disagree with those frightening predictions.

THE REAL DEAL IS -- Earth has experienced other warming phases which have been much warmer than now and it's never become uninhabitable, much less destroyed.

WARM WEATHER? ...COOL!

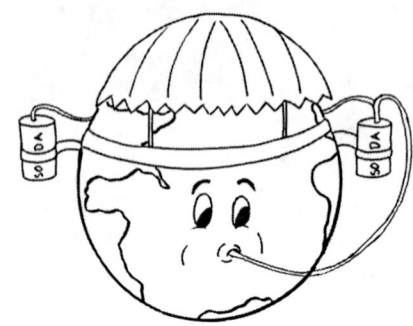

Even though earth has been warmer in the past we keep hearing about it like it's the first time ever. And this time it will be like...

THE END OF THE WORLD!

The end of the world is clearly not what happened when earth became warmer in the past. We know this because we're still here! And why all the panic about a warmer climate, when history tells us that earth's past warm phases were actually pretty cool! (That's cool, as in great, not cool as in cold).

During the Medieval Warm Period, not only did the temperature elevate, but so did the quality of people's lives. There were fewer storms and fewer floods, and the new sunny climate brought great prosperity!

| PROSPERITY - Wealth, success, riches. |

During this time Vikings were able to travel by boat and explore places outside of Northern Europe. Earlier they were unable to prosper in these locations because the colder weather and the icy waters prevented it. Farmers also gained a new sunny outlook on life, as agriculture flourished and they were able to sell more food and wine.

Today we hear that a warmer earth would mean catastrophe for us, but it sounds like the warm weather trend of the Medieval Warm Period made a lot of medieval folks, pretty happy!

Think about it...

Isn't it nice to know that we can totally chill out about all the scary things we hear about global warming? Warming and cooling on earth is not new, so it is not our fault. It's natural for earth.

CHAPTER 2

THE REAL DEAL ON MAN-MADE GLOBAL WARMING

GREENHOUSE GASES

WE HEAR…

People are the biggest, nastiest greenhouse gas polluters, ever!!

We're told that earth is heating up super fast, sea levels will rise, cities will flood, animals will become extinct, and guess who is getting the blame?

That's right, us! You, me, your mom, your dad, your sister, your brother, your … Well you get the picture. We're told that our planet is getting hotter because of all the greenhouse gases we all produce.

But what are greenhouse gases??

Greenhouse gases are gases that absorb infrared radiation in the atmosphere. These gases include water vapor, carbon dioxide, methane, nitrous oxide, halogenated fluorocarbons (HCFCs), ozone, perfluorinated carbons (PFCs), and hydrofluorocarbons (HFCs).

HYDROFLUOROCARBONS!!
PERFLUORINATED CARBONS!?
HALOGENATED FLUROCARBONS?!

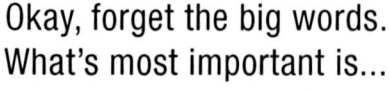

Okay, forget the big words. What's most important is...

HUMANS CAUSE VERY LITTLE GREEN HOUSE GAS!

Yet we're told we're big time, global warming polluters of the stuff, especially a dastardly gas called "carbon dioxide", (or CO^2). But just how dastardly is CO^2? Is it really a scary, planet-killer, or is there a very different side to CO^2 that we don't hear:

> The more CO^2 there is, the more plant growth there is.
>
> Food production around the world has increased 16% because of extra CO^2.
>
> CO2 is not even a pollutant!
>
> AND...
>
> All green vegetation must have CO^2 to live and give off oxygen as a by-product so we can all live!

OXYGEN - An odorless, colorless gas that makes up 21 percent of earth's atmosphere. Oxygen is necessary for most forms of life and is absorbed through the lungs into the blood.

CARBON DIOXIDE - A colorless, odorless, tasteless, non-toxic gas which is essential to all life on earth!!

Although we need CO2 to live we're told that we create too much by using electricity, making things in our factories,

and driving in our cars.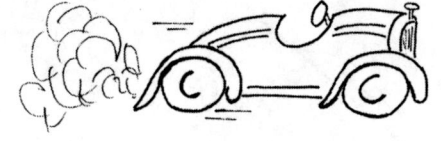

But how can that be when there were other times in earth's past, long before electricity, factories and cars when CO2 levels were **HIGHER** than they are today?

So where did all <u>that</u> CO2 come from??

THE REAL DEAL IS, CO2 is only a tiny part of greenhouse gases, and the amount of CO2 caused by humans is even tinier than that! Most CO2 (and greenhouse gases) come from natural sources like decaying leaves and the ocean.

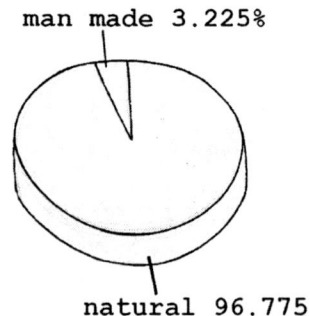

This means, even if we all stopped using electricity, making things in our factories,

and driving in our cars

It wouldn't make much of a difference at all. It would only get rid of CO2 by only a teeny bit!!

THE REAL DEAL IS -- Greenhouse gases include CO2. But CO2 is actually one of the smallest elements that make up greenhouse gases.

HUMAN'S AREN'T THE BOSS OF EARTH!

Why is it that when we see changes in the earth's climate humans get the blame?

Why don't we see this as the natural event that it is? And most of all, why are we so freaked out and worried that we must...

STOP GLOBAL WARMING, NOW

...especially when

THE REAL DEAL IS, no one really even knows how to make climate *chill-ax* in the first place? We're simply not that powerful!

Think about how powerless we really are...

Could a human change how much heat the sun puts out? Build a mountain range? Create a desert? Keep the rain forest rainy? Fill an ocean, or drain one dry?

How about, stop an oncoming tornado?

ABSO-TIVELY POSI-TUTELY NOT!

We can't even figure out how to stop weeds from popping up in our gardens year after year. How could we possibly stop something as complex and out of our control as global climate? Earth does all this cool stuff without any help from us and it always has. Humans simply aren't the boss of earth.

EARTH IS AWESOME!

What if humans really were the boss of earth?

Well, when it comes to global warming it sounds like we have all kinds of super-hero abilities with total control of the world. We hear stuff like...

WE CAN PREDICT FUTURE CLIMATE!

    WE CAN PREDICT HOW EARTH WILL BE DESTROYED!

        WE CAN WARM THE EARTH AND COOL IT DOWN!

But **THE REAL DEAL IS**, we cannot do any of those things!

Think about how powerful the earth is...

First there were bacteria, then multi-cellular life, then great seas.

Then came land creatures including dinosaurs that lasted millions and millions of years.

Gigantic mountain ranges sprang up, then ice, wind and water carved them into the majestic and curious formations we see today.

There were volcanic explosions.

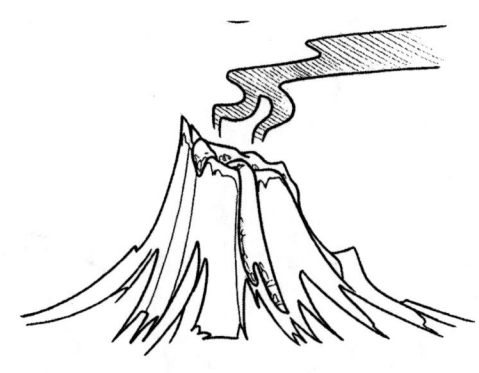

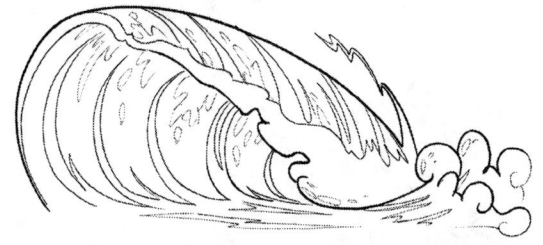

Oceans grew larger and shrunk smaller.

Whole continents moved and changed. Even today, mountain ranges including the Rocky Mountains are still getting bigger!

Earth gets warmer, colder, wetter, drier, stormier, calmer, you name it, all by itself. And this has gone on for millions of years without any help from humans.

So, if this is earth doing what earth does, how on earth are we to believe that something as perfect and powerful and incredibly amazing as earth can be destroyed by leaving our microwave plugged in, or saved by switching to a goofy looking light bulb?

Think about it...

Climate change is one of the natural, miraculous things that make planet earth such an amazing creation!

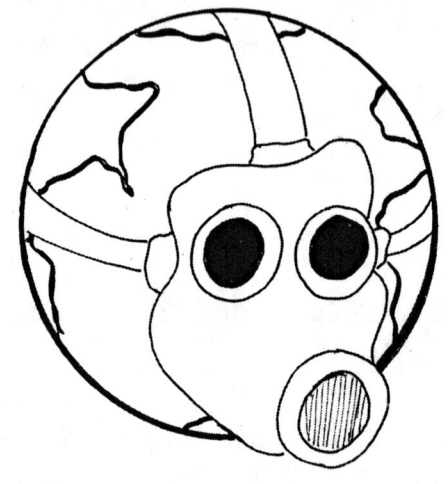

CHAPTER 3

GREENHOUSE GASES & EARTH

MAN VS. VOLCANOES

WE HEAR...

Greenhouse gases are all man's fault!

Man is BAD BAD BAD!!

When it comes to global warming we hear a lot about terrible, no-good, greenhouse gases. But what we don't hear is that greenhouse gases are pretty important. In fact they are necessary for life on earth.

Another thing we rarely hear when it comes to greenhouse gases is that the total man-made greenhouse gas contributions only add up to 0.28% of the greenhouse effect. That's 0.28%, way less than 1 percent!   Although we keep hearing that man is guilty, human activities like farming, manufacturing, power generation and transportation only add a tiny bit to greenhouse gases.

So, where do the other greenhouse gases come from?

Greenhouse gases cycle naturally through the earth's atmosphere, land masses and oceans. For instance, **GINORMOUS** amounts are absorbed into the atmosphere during volcanic eruptions.

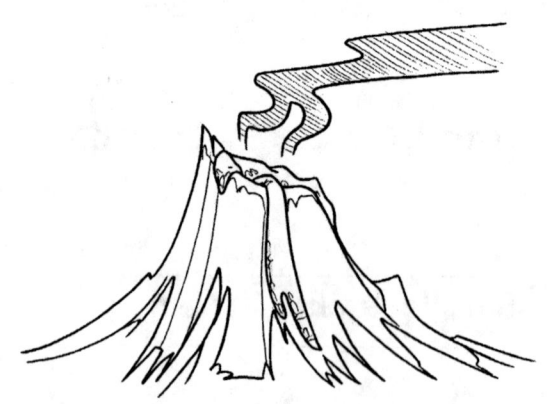

THE REAL DEAL IS -- when Mount Pinatubo erupted it put more gunk in the air than all the car exhaust in the history of cars!

VAPOR & SUNSHINE & BEASTS, OH MY!

Some animals and insects also contribute more greenhouse gases into the atmosphere than humans, like moose and termites. Wood-feeding termites digest their fiber-rich food and emit another very potent greenhouse gas, called methane.

By the way, methane is a much larger and more powerful element of greenhouse gas than CO2, but let's **MOOOOOVE** on to the subject of cows. Did you know that the fiber that cows chew is later emitted into the atmosphere as methane when they *burp* and "*poot*"?

POOT - An episode of flatulance.

FLATULENCE - A mixture of gases that are produced by symbiotic bacteria and yeasts living in the gastrointestinal tract of mammals, and it is released under pressure with a characteristic sound and odor. Flatulence is known colloquially as farting.

BURP - A reflex that expels wind noisily from the stomach through the mouth.

Although man's activities are always blamed, these gaseous livestock polluters are responsible for 18% of greenhouse gases in the atmosphere. They produce five times more than cars, trucks, airplanes, and all other forms of transportation put together!

THE REAL DEAL IS -- Studies have found a lot more natural contributors to greenhouse gases far outweigh human contributors.

The roughly 86 million cattle in the United States produce about several million metric tons of methane into the atmosphere annually.

Another place we can look to find greenhouse gases and why earth gets warmer and cooler is right above our heads because 95 % of greenhouse gas is water vapor. Water vapor is the most important greenhouse gas and overwhelms all other man-made and natural greenhouse gas contributors put together.

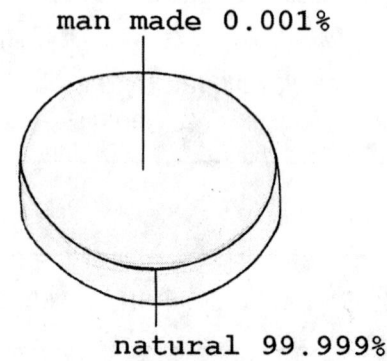

21

And here's something else that's rarely heard

THE REAL DEAL IS, clouds and the sun may play a huge role in this whole global warming issue.

For years, scientists all over the world believed that more sunspots (on the sun) brought warmer weather (on the earth).

And when these scientists checked it out further they found out that solar activity closely matches what happens to earth's temperature change over the last 100 years. Even 400 years of astronomical records found the same thing! That means it seems as if the sun, **NOT CARBON DIOXIDE**, could be the real boss of the earth's temperature.

THE REAL DEAL IS -- during the Little Ice Age there were barely any sunspots visible on the sun.

... AND THE WINNER OF THE MOST INTERESTING FACT ABOUT CO2 GOES TO...

Ice core records show that higher CO2 levels increase AFTER temperature rises, not BEFORE! So carbon dioxide can't be the reason that temperature rises! This means, whether we make more CO2 or cut back in future, it won't much matter in terms of the climate.

THE REAL DEAL IS --This one scientific fact totally contradicts what the global warming alarmists tell us about man-made global warming and its solutions!

CHAPTER 4

INDUSTRY & GLOBAL WARMING

THE REAL DEAL ON INDUSTRY

WE HEAR...

Industry's the problem!

Industry is bad!

Use less industry!

Or earth will be sad!

When it comes to global warming we're told that we are warming our planet because of our use of industry (making products in factories). But that argument pretty much fizzles out when we look at the history of industry and the history of earth's past warming trends.

INDUSTRY - The organized action of producing goods and services for sale. During the 19th Century innovations in technology led to steam engines, factories and mass production.

THE REAL DEAL IS -- Any recent global warming hasn't even been as warm as the warmest temperature during the Medieval Warm Period, long before industry. The Holocene Maximum (a warming period before the Medieval Warm period) was the warmest period in the last 10,000 years.

In fact, in the last 10,000 years, the warmest periods have all happened well before humans developed factories. Yet humans and their factories are getting blamed big time for warming the earth, even though during the Industrial Revolution (between 1940–1977 when lots of products were being manufactured in our factories), the earth actually cooled!

Some of the many things manufactured between 1940-1977

JEEP
COLOR TV
COMPUTER
SPRAY CAN
TURBOPROP ENGINE
SYNTHETIC RUBBER
THE SLINKY
KIDNEY DIALYSIS
SILLY PUTTY
TUPPERWARE
BIKINI
MICROWAVE OVEN
TRANSISTOR RADIO
FRISBEE
MOBILE PHONE
JUKEBOX
VELCRO
CREDIT CARDS

DIET SODA
POWER STEERING
VIDEO TAPE RECORDER
RADIAL TIRES
SYNTHESIZER
McDONALDS
NON-STICK PANS
TETRACYALINE
OPTIC FIBER
MODEM
SEAT BELTS
SATELLITE
LASER
HULA HOOP
PACEMAKER
BARBIE
MICROCHIP
HALOGEN LAMP
VIDEO GAME
VIDEO DISC

ACRYLIC PAINT
PERMA PRESS FABRIC
ASTROTURF
CONTACT LENSES
KEVLAR
CD
HANDHELD COMPUTER
COMPUTER MOUSE
RAM
ARTIFICIAL HEART
ATM
FLOPPY DISC
INTERNET
BAR-CODE SCANNER
LCD
VCR

If our current use of industry is truly the biggest reason the earth is warming, then the earth would have stayed consistently cool up to the age of industry and then warmed. But that's not the case.

1940-1975 - The planet cooled!

1975-1998 – The planet warmed!

1998 – The planetary average shows essentially no warming!

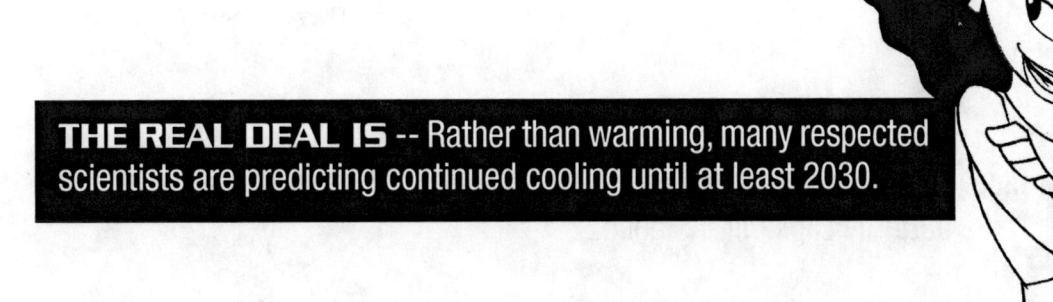

THE REAL DEAL IS -- Rather than warming, many respected scientists are predicting continued cooling until at least 2030.

INDUSTRY, SO COOL!

Trends come and go.

TREND - to extend in a general direction; follow a general course.

Some trends are cool, some not so cool...
like butterfly clips, for instance.

Okay! They're gone! Yeesh!

Another not so cool trend is how it's become "trendy" to be against industry.

Unfortunately, a lot of what we hear about global warming comes from radical environmental groups who promote this anti-industry trend. They believe that industry and the way we live on earth is the cause of global warming, so they want industry stopped or drastically reduced. But **THE REAL DEAL IS**, their beliefs are as incorrect as their solutions are impractical …and radical!

RADICAL - favoring drastic political, economic, or social reforms: radical ideas; radical and anarchistic ideologues. Person who holds or follows strong convictions or extreme principles; extremist.

One of their solutions to get rid of global warming is to live more like we did before the industrial revolution when we were still doing all of our work ourselves, or with the help of horses, instead of using fossil fuels and machinery.

Serious?

Think about how hard your life would be without industry...

A time machine! cool!

It would be like stepping back in time!

Huh?!

Without modern technology there would be no electricity. That means no television, no lights and no computers (which also means no favorite shows, no staying up late, and no computer games)!

It would be super hard to cool down in the summer because there wouldn't be any air conditioning. Fortunately, in the winter you could stay nice and toasty. But, first you'd have to go outside in the cold and gather or chop wood to burn for heat. Your indoor heat would not come from a home heating system like you have now, but from a wood burning stove. This means to stay warm you and your whole family would have to stay in the same room as the stove.

Also, since there would be no electricity, there would be no way to sanitize water to drink, which could make you dreadfully sick (and that's if you're lucky).

Water for your bath, would have to be heated on the wood burning stove. But first you'd have to bring it in from an outside well… **one bucket at a time.**

Something tells me this is going to take a looong time!

And how do you think you would get to school?

Well, in the rain, or snow or blazing heat you'd be riding in a horse drawn buggy, because before industry this was the only form of transportation.

Without electricity there would be no washing machines or dryers, you would also have to wash your clothes by hand in a bucket or a hand-cranked tub and hang them outside to dry.

But look on the bright side. You'd only have one or two outfits to wash because without modern technology clothes would not be mass produced, and affordable, and available at your favorite stores like they are now.

Now imagine the total picture.

You buggy home from school, chop wood, pull water from a well, lug it inside, heat it on a stove, hand-wash your clothes and do your homework by candlelight and there is something much worse .. **Much, much worse!**

What could be worse than this?

Serious?

There would be no indoor bathrooms!

So, although it might be a popular trend to be against industry the reality is, without it our lives wouldn't be nearly as fun, easy, clean and cool as it is with industry.

Let me out of here!

THE REAL DEAL IS -- Industry allows us to live easier, healthier, longer, and more efficient lives; to prosper and look forward to an even better future. Wealthier is healthier and cleaner!

Sadly some environmental activist groups that promote this anti-industry idea have a lot of influence on our government, businesses, how we live our lives, and what we believe about issues concerning earth.

ACTIVIST - Extensively and vigorously involved in political activity, either within or outside the governmental system; militant reform.

RADICAL - favoring drastic political, economic, or social reforms: radical ideas; radical and anarchistic ideologues. Person who holds or follows strong convictions or extreme principles; extremist.

And since they believe that earth should forever be industry-free, fossil fuels is their sworn enemy.

FOSSIL FUELS - Carbon based sources of energy such as coal, oil, and natural gas. Fossil fuels provide energy demands for heating, transportation, electricity generation, and other uses.

But right now (and as far as we can tell about the future) we need fossil fuels. We need them every day to make electricity, run our cars and trucks (which by the way, helps the economy grow!). And fossil fuels will be necessary to find and make other cleaner methods of energy!

THE REAL DEAL IS -- Industry allows humans to live longer and more fulfilling lives. But industry is the big enemy of radical environmentalists.

Man, they don't like anything!

Currently there are other ways for us to generate electricity like power dams and nuclear power plants. But these groups fight against us having those things too.

Not only do they fight against building energy resources in developed countries (like the United States), but in poor, under-developed countries too! And what happens to them as a result of not having needed technology is totally not cool.

THE REAL DEAL IS -- Radical environmental activist groups are not to be mistaken with all environmental groups. Some environmental groups care about the earth, but also care about the well-being of people, first.

IF INDUSTRY IS SO BAD, WHY DOES THE REST OF THE WORLD WANT IT?

Sadly, some pretty powerful activist groups have had a lot of influence in keeping poor people in underdeveloped countries from having modern technology. The sad result is, this pretty much guarantees they will not only remain poor, but also unhealthy.

But **THE REAL DEAL IS**, poor people want modern technology and they need it to help improve their daily lives.

Let's check it out!

95% of people in sub-Saharan Africa still do not have electricity, or they only get electricity just a few hours every week or two, and they never know in advance when they will get it!

In Uganda, activists are trying to stop a hydroelectric dam from being built. A hydroelectric dam would bring renewable electricity to millions of Africans. Without it they have no electricity in their shops, schools and hospitals!

Whoa! No electricity? how do they live?

Think about this...

THE REAL DEAL IS -- Without industry and modern technology these poor people have very difficult lives. They must use only the sun for light which means when the sun goes down, their day is over.

With no electricity in their hospitals there's no way to refrigerate food for patients. There's no way to keep medications cool to prevent them from spoiling. There are no computers to get hospital records from, and there's no way their doctors can use modern, medical technology like our doctors use. Also, no electricity means, no safe, clean, water. Without sanitized water it makes it super hard for their doctors to fight diseases and save their lives.

Forced to live without electricity in their homes they cook and heat their house by cutting trees, and gathering and drying animal dung by hand, which they burn inside their homes like a campfire. Because they must breathe in the smoke and pollution from these fires every day many mothers and young children get lung infections and simply don't survive.

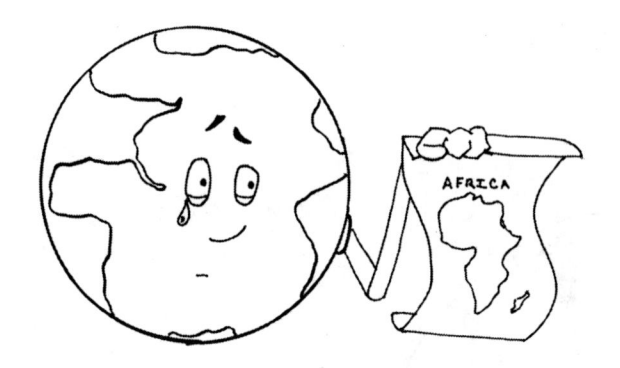

Think of how much you'd like to live like this.

Sadly, the health and well-being of the poorest people on our planet is most affected by them not having modern technology. Nevertheless, many activist environmental groups approve of this way of life for them because after all, they're not contributing to global warming!

THE REAL DEAL IS -- If democracy, industry and modern technology for the poor were fought for and promoted, the planet would actually be cleaner. The places where they live would have less poverty and these people would have more productive, healthy and safer lives!

DEMOCRACY - The term democracy indicates a form of government where all the state's decisions are exercised directly or indirectly by a majority of its citizenry through a fair elective process.

THE REAL DEAL IS -- Richer countries have technology to manufacture products for cleaner air. But the poorest countries have the largest population growth, which puts more stress on the environment. Wealthier is healthier!

"What gives the developed nations the right to make choices for the poor?"
-- James Skikwati, Economist - Kenya

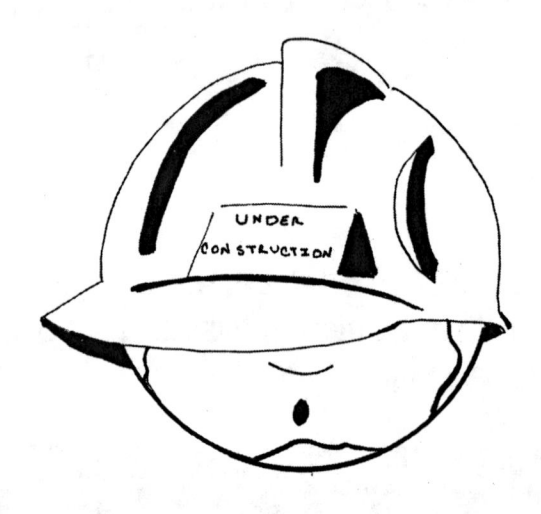

CHAPTER 5

DON'T WORRY EARTH! WE'LL FIX YOU!

FOLLOW THE LEADER!

WE HEAR…

You must save the earth!

It's your duty!!

But, let's check it out!

We hear that humans are the cause of global warming which makes us responsible for fixing it, and fast! Young and old, big and small we must all do our part because (as we're told) this is the most serious matter of our time. We should immediately start to do things like unplug our microwaves, bike, use goofy looking light bulbs, plant trees, wear warmer clothes, walk instead of drive, and by all means...

ONLY USE COLD WATER!!

Is.s.s this r.r.r really s.s.saving the planet?

But if you check out what some of the leaders of the global warming movement are doing, you might be surprised. While some of them tell us that **WE** should cut our use of fossil fuels and drastically simplify our lives **THEY** live quite extravagantly and take private jets all around the world. Some of them have **GINORMOUS** household electric bills, bigger than any of ours 20-200 times over!

FOSSIL FUELS - Carbon based sources of energy such as coal, oil, and natural gas. Fossil fuels provide energy demands such as heating, transportation, electricity generation, and other uses.

One popular global warming leader uses more electricity in a week than 28 million Ugandans put together use in a year. Another well-known celebrity who tells us what sacrifices we should make to stop global warming has a 4,000 square foot,

"Jet Do As I Say, Not as I Do"

air conditioned farm!

So what's up with this "do as I say, not as I do" behavior? We're told they're entitled to their GINORMOUS use of electricity and fossil fuels because they're getting the message out about global warming. You know the message, the one about how the rest of us have to use less electricity and fossil fuels!

THE REAL DEAL IS -- Leaders of the global warming movement tell us that we must live more simply, but many of them are still taking private jets and limousines all over the world. If global warming is as destructive to the earth as they say, don't they owe it to the earth to stop traveling that way?

W.w.wait! Why are t.t.they the b.b.boss of us?!

CARBON UP-SETS

> **!!POP QUIZ!!**
>
> **Question:** Who creates a problem that wasn't a problem in the first place then creates the solution to the problem that wasn't a problem in the first place that will cost us a ton of money to fix, even though the problem wasn't a problem in the first place?
>
> **Answer:** The Global Warming Movement

The more we hear about global warming, the more we hear about the solutions to global warming.

Unfortunately, most of the solutions would continue to force poor people in under developed countries to remain poor, and people in developed countries (like the U.S.) would have to change their personal energy habits big time!... Or pay a big time price!

Let's check it out!

One popular solution to global warming is called, carbon off-setting which would have us pay for what we personally contribute to global warming (called our "carbon footprint").

> **CARBON OFFSETS** – Payment to a person or organization to remove the guilt about personal "carbon footprints". Often trees are planted with this money to "off-set" the amount of fossil fuels someone uses.

> **CARBON FOOTPRINT** – A calculation of the CO_2 emissions each person is responsible for, either directly because of his or her transportation and energy consumption, or indirectly because of the manufacture and eventual breakdown of products he or she uses.

If you want to know how many of these "footprints" you actually make and how much it'll cost, don't worry. The price will be determined by the carbon offset company!

> **THE REAL DEAL IS** -- Carbon offsets is an easy payment for the wealthy, like Hollywood celebrities, but it could be terribly costly and harmful economically for the average person or family.

Okay, so carbon offsetting sounds like they're charging people to live on earth (okay, they are charging people to live on earth!), but at least it offers a way to help people feel really good about themselves. At least they can rest assured that they are personally helping to save the earth…

…**NOT!!**

THE REAL DEAL IS -- "Offsetting" does nothing to cut down on supposedly damaging human emissions because people who pay this fee never have to change their energy habits. So in reality, even if they could, they're not doing anything to help save the earth.

If you ask me it's more like carbon upsetting.

CFL LIGHTBULBS

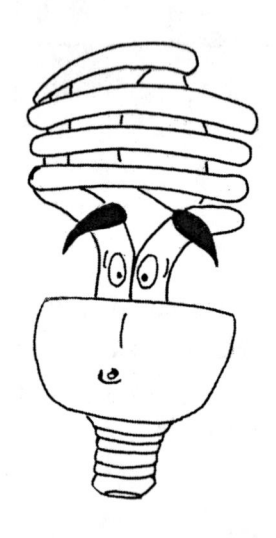

& WHATNOT

Another new popular "earth-saving fix" is the compact fluorescent light bulb (or CFL). CFL bulbs look a little funnier (okay, a lot funnier) and they cost a little more (okay a lot more), and because of growing global warming fears we all may have to throw out our regular bulbs and use them because we're told they're going to help...

SAVE THE WORLD!!!

They're also supposed to **save energy** *(over time)*, and **save us money**

(over time) and **save us from being chased by monsters** *(over time)*!
Okay, maybe we haven't heard they can save us from monsters, but we're also not

"Let's check it out!"

hearing the total **REAL DEAL** about them, either!

First off, it's reported that these bulbs are only **"safe when used correctly"**. They cannot be used with dimmers or even in some track lighting without causing a potential fire hazard.

"**If it starts blinking on you, take it out. Don't wait for it to stop. If it fails and you see it failing, disconnect the power immediately.**"

- Electrical Safety Authority

"Gulp!"

Also they contain small amounts of mercury, and with some cities already making these bulbs mandatory there's going to be lots of them to deal with, and no real practical way to throw them away!

MERCURY - a silver-white poisonous heavy metallic element that is liquid at ordinary temperatures and is used especially in batteries, in dental amalgam, and in scientific instruments.

THE REAL DEAL IS -- A single CFL bulb contains six times the state of Maine's "safe" level of mercury.

For the safety of their trash workers, some cities have made it illegal for us to put CFL bulbs in trash cans altogether because they can break in containers, or dumpsters, or in trash trucks before they get to the landfill.

What happens if I drop one??

THE REAL DEAL IS, there are differences of opinions over how dangerous mercury actually is. But there's one thing for sure, if you drop one of these babies, it doesn't sound "good"! A woman in Maine accidentally broke one that shattered on her carpet. Check out what happened to her when she tried the professional method.

THE PROFESSIONAL METHOD

- She called the store where she bought it...

- The store told her to call the Poison Control hotline...

- The Poison Control Hotline told her to contact the Department of Environmental Protection...

- Environmental Protection sent a specialist to her house to test for mercury contamination...

- The specialist found the levels of mercury were in excess and recommended that she call an environmental clean up firm...

And finally...

- The environmental clean up firm cleaned the room for a fee of $2,000.00!!!

But don't you worry. If you drop one you don't have to go the professional route. There's always the **do-it-yourself** method.

THE DO-IT-YOURSELF METHOD

- Don't vacuum it because the vacuum will spread mercury containing dust and contaminate the vacuum cleaner...

- Ventilate the area and reduce the temperature...

- Wear protective equipment like goggles, coveralls, gloves and a dust mask...

- Collect the waste material from the bulb and put it in an airtight container...

- Pat the area where it dropped with a sticky side of tape to collect anything you can't see...

- Wipe over the area with a damp cloth...

- Put the damp cloth in the airtight container when you're finished...

- Find out where you can safely throw the airtight container away...

  And finally...

- Immediately, call the authorities to see if you've cleaned it all up...which will cost you a fee!

I repeat...gulp!

THE REAL DEAL IS -- The vast, over-whelming majority of carbon comes from natural sources. So even if the most costly, dangerous or ridiculous efforts to limit human emissions worked, they would have a very small and most likely undetectable effect on global climate.

...AND THE WINNER OF THE WACKIEST GLOBAL WARMING SOLUTION YET GOES TO...

To combat global warming one group suggests creating an artificial ring of small particles around the Earth. Unfortunately, they admit there would be side effects, like completely lighting up the night sky and costing all of us 6 trillion to 200 trillion dollars!

CHAPTER 6

WHY DOES IT SEEM SO REAL?!

BOO!!

WE HEAR...

I Believe...

You Believe...

We all believe...

In Global Warming!

When it comes to the global warming movement it seems like almost everyone has become instant believers. But have you ever thought about how so many people came to believe in something they know so little about?

Let's check it out!

Advertisers sometimes use fun cartoon characters to get us to buy their brands of breakfast cereals. Well, global warming "advertisers" sell us their ideas on global warming, too.

But they don't use fun cartoons. For the most part, they use fearful images that scare the dickens out of us!

APOCALYPSE!   CATASTROPHE!   DDDDOOM!

This fear technique works the same as when we ride a really gnarly roller coaster, or

It's only a movie...
It's only a movie...
It's only a movie..

watch a freakishly spooky zombie movie.

Even though deep down you know you're not in any real danger, your mind gets carried

Let me out of here!

away and you buy into it anyway.

Think about what we hear about global warming...

MASSIVE FLOODS!   TERRIBLE STORMS!

CREEPY DISEASES!

THE REAL DEAL IS, Most of us are simply scared into believing what we hear. But who wouldn't be afraid? All that stuff sounds pretty scary and very, very real! But guess what? This is an old trick! Fear tactics simply aren't new when it comes to environmental issues. Scary predictions made by environmental alarmists have been going on for a long, long time.

ALARMIST - A person who alarms others needlessly.

Not long ago, people were told that half of all animal species would be extinct by now because of chemicals, the oceans couldn't be saved, hair spray would destroy ozone, and literally billions of humans would be erased from the planet because of mass starvation. And people totally freaked out about those things then, just like we're freaking out about global warming now.

THE REAL DEAL IS, fear freezes you and me. We can't make logical decisions about what to do about anything when we're frozen with fear.

Sadly, today's global warming alarmists still continue to spread their doomsday message, without regard to their past wrong prediction[s] respected scientists who are trying to get the word out and t[o] that all these terrible, scary events are highly unlikely to ha[ppen].

THE REAL DEAL IS -- The global warming scare has worked. Predictions of certain doom have convinced a lot of people by appealing to their emotions, not their logic.

I'm scarier than both of you. I'm a global warming alarmist!

"THE MOST SERIOUS ISSUE OF OUR TIME"!

"Global warming… It's the most serious issue of our time."

-- U. S. TV Commercial
(2007, the U.S. is at war)

If changing climate is typical earth behavior, and it's not a demonstrated fact that we can affect it, how on earth can it possibly be "the **MOST** serious issue of our time"?

Well, **THE REAL DEAL IS**, over-exaggerating the facts is a large part of how the global warming issue works!

Let's check it out!

EXAGGERATION - the act of making something more noticeable than usual; making something seem more important than it really is.

Sea level rise? Bring it on!

A popular movie on global warming says that potential melting ice sheets in Greenland and West Antarctic will experience a sea level rise of 6 meters (20 feet) and force millions of people to…

EVACUATE!

RUN!

HEAD FOR THE HILLS!

But most research says that, even if it could occur, melting ice caps and rising sea levels would take 1,000 to 5,000 years to happen!

Now what am I supposed to do with all this stuff?

THE REAL DEAL IS -- It's easy to make something the biggest issue of our time when you exaggerate!

NO ESCAPE!

Another reason all those scary, doomsday messages about global warming are so believable is because of "repetition". Look around! The whole "global-warming-bringing-about-major-catastrophe" theme is presented in our movies, commercials, talk shows, schools, books, billboards, documentaries, websites, comic books, magazines… Well you get the picture. It's everywhere! It's no wonder global warming seems like it's an accepted fact these days!

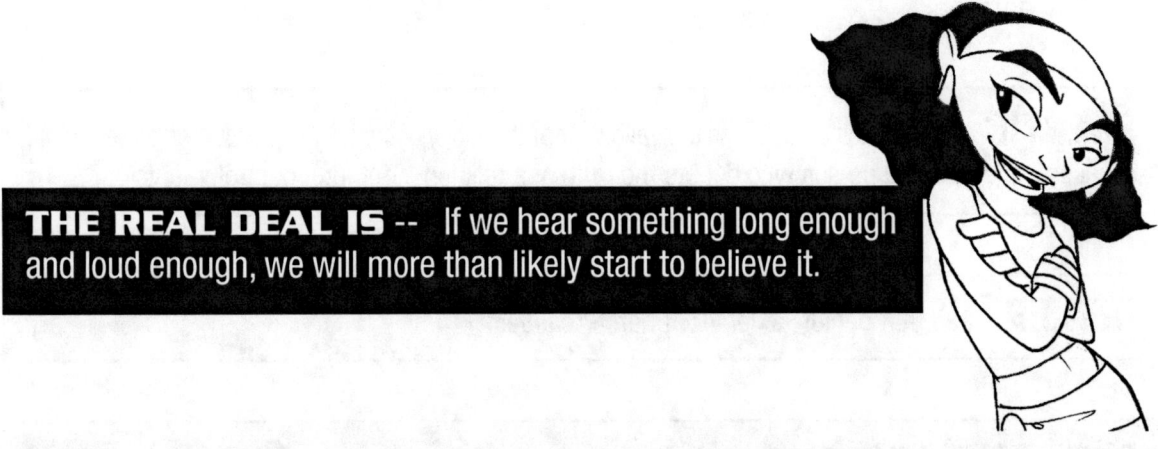

THE REAL DEAL IS -- If we hear something long enough and loud enough, we will more than likely start to believe it.

Sadly, too many of us won't do the work to find out the other side of this issue for ourselves (of course, not you, because you're reading this book!).

No thanks, I'd rather freak out

STICKS AND STONES

"Sticks and stones may break my bones, but names can never hurt me."

- Author Unknown

Name-calling may not physically hurt like sticks and stones, but it doesn't exactly inspire you to speak up, either! Unfortunately, many people who challenge the popular views on global warming are often called names like "skeptics", "deniers" and "flat-earthers".

SKEPTIC - A person who questions the validity or authenticity of something purporting to be factual; also used to describe a person who doubts the truth of a religion, or of important elements of it.

DENIER - One that denies: a denier of harsh realities.

FLAT-EARTHER - A person who is so behind the times they still believe that the earth is flat.

They're even told that "all moral people" agree with today's global warming views. So, does this mean that people who don't agree with global warming are "immoral"?

IMMORAL - Deliberately violating accepted principles of right and wrong. Bad: wicked.

Okay, rude!

THE REAL DEAL IS -- if global warming is supposed to be the most important issue of our time and its solutions are supposed to save the world, shouldn't we at least be having an open, honest discussion (or even a nice chat) about it without name calling?

ZIP IT!

If there's another side to global warming, have you ever wondered why you rarely hear it?

THE REAL DEAL IS -- There are many opposing views to global warming!

Fortunately, there are many respected scientists, researchers and professors from all over the world who strongly disagree with popular global warming views and its catastrophic effects on the planet. Unfortunately, they are simply not being heard. Instead, they're called names, told that there is "no debate" on this topic and there's no need to talk about it in the first place because there is "consensus" on this matter.

CONSENSUS - A consensus implies that debate has taken place, the solution is generally accepted rather than a compromise. That agreement is deep-rooted enough to stand for some time without need to revisit the issue.

THE REAL DEAL IS -- "Beliefs" don't equal "facts" any more than "consensus" equals "scientific proof".

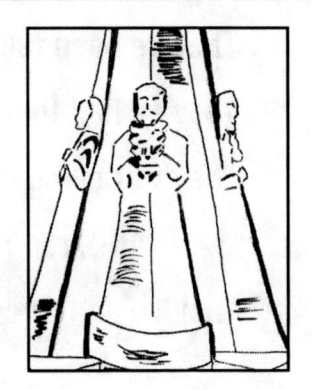

But this way of shutting people up is a very old technique. Because Galileo disagreed with the "consensus" of his time (in 1633), he was ordered to stand trial for saying the Earth was not the center of the universe. There was no debating this matter then either. He was given a choice between being tortured or burned alive at the stake if he didn't "zip it". Galileo went with "zip it", but they placed him under house arrest for the rest of his life, anyway.

Okay, rude!

By the way, later Galileo was proven to be right!

THE REAL DEAL IS -- Just because something is popular doesn't make it right!

These days, people who disagree with the "consensus" of global warming catastrophic prophecies aren't burned alive, or put under house arrest, but they are silenced in other ways. They're generally not invited to discuss their views on the news, talk shows, popular newspapers, magazines, or in schools which means, we're only getting one side of the story.

There have been some very brave scientists, researchers and professors who have tried to openly question claims of rapid global warming, man's impact on climate change, and catastrophic predictions due to global warming, but like Galileo, they have also paid a really tough price.

- They've been rejected by others in their field.
- They've had their research money disappear.
- They've been falsely accused of working for big oil companies.
- They've had their research work ridiculed
- They've been called "fools", "stooges", "climate criminals"
    - AND, LAST BUT NOT LEAST…
- They've had threats against their lives and the lives of their families.

With this amount of hostility, it's no wonder many people choose not to loudly disagree or choose to "zip it" altogether. The bad news is, by successfully quieting the majority of well respected people like these, the horror story of global warming has caught on like wild fire.

Think about it...

How on earth can science advance if all scientific knowledge was "given" and then forbidden to be questioned and proved? Sadly this is what's going on with global warming when many of the best and brightest have been told to **"zip it!"**

CHAPTER 7

WHO'S TELLING US THIS SCARY STUFF AND WHY?

THE MEDIA

WE HEAR…

Take our word

We know the deal

Listen to us

Global warming is real!

If you're like me, you've probably got some really cool people in your life. People you can trust to tell you the truth and give you great information on all kinds of stuff. But where are we getting the information on global warming from? And why does it all sound so scary?

Let's check it out!

THE REAL DEAL IS, we get most of the global warming message from the media.

> **MEDIA** - Any form of information, including television news, printed news, documentaries, television specials, talk shows, movies and music. "Mass media" is specifically conceived and designed to reach a very large audience.

The media and the global warming movement are like total best friends. Where you find one, you're bound to find the other. One reason is because scary, menacing, terrifying stories about global warming help the media make lots and lots of money!

The media isn't just to inform and entertain us, it's a business, and its main purpose is to make money. It makes money by getting lots and lots of viewers. And the way they get lots and lots of viewers is by making what they present sound very, very exciting. If the media features global warming alarmists the program sounds pretty exciting!

"Fire!" *"Disaster!"*
"Flood!"
"Apocalypse!" *"Doom!"*

On the other hand, if they feature people who don't agree with global warming alarmists, the program may sound pretty much like this... **Z..z..z..z..z..z..z..**.

> **!!POP QUIZ!!**
> (Don't worry, it's easy)
>
> **What's a more exciting news story?**
> A) "Earth only has one last week to survive! Run! Hide! Kiss your dog goodbye!"
> B) "Earth will no doubt continue to do what it has always done. Everything's fine."
>
> **Right, A!** (Told you it was a no-brainer. It's a no-brainer for the media, too!)

THE REAL DEAL IS, Stories about global warming disaster are very profitable for the media and apparently the wilder the story, the better. They love the stuff! This is why big natural weather events like Hurricane Katrina and other big hurricanes in Florida, Louisiana and Texas were quickly blamed on global warming. Even though there was no evidence to prove this, the media reported it as fact.

Another likely reason media helps the global warming movement is because many people who work in the media are believers of the popular global warming view themselves. Naturally, this topic is important to them. So global warming stories are presented as real news and indisputable facts but **THE REAL DEAL IS**, many times these stories are simply glitzy productions of the media's own "personal" beliefs. Because of this we're not being given information about global warming from a well-debated, well-thought-through, fair and balanced view of it.

HOLLYWOOD WACK-A-DO'S

Another group that helps get the word out about global warming is Hollywood.

Have you ever noticed how celebrities tend to give advice on really important stuff? Well...

They're baaaack!

Movie stars, TV stars and music artists, as far as the eye can see, passionately warn us about global warming and tell us how to solve it. But are they the best people to follow in matters as important and costly as this?

Let's check it out!

DUMB HOLLYWOOD QUOTES

"What's Wal-Mart, do they sell like wall stuff?"
--Paris Hilton

"I feel my best when I'm happy."
--Winona Ryder

"If I could read a book, I'd definitely read one of yours."
-- Paris Hilton

(When asked whether he had visited the Parthenon in Greece)
"I can't really remember the names of the clubs that we went to."
--Shaquille O'Neal

"It's not that I dislike many people. It's just that I don't like many people."
-- Bryant Gumbel

"A zebra does not change its spots"
-- Al Gore
(1991 and again in 1992)

Sounds like someone forgot to pay their brain bill!

Some stars are very admirable. They exhibit common sense, character, self-control and commitment. As for the others, maybe it's smarter for us to enjoy their talent, not let them influence our opinions on ideas that seriously affect our lives.

SCHOOLS

Most teachers are committed to teaching us valuable academic skills (you know the kind of stuff that helps insure our future success like learn to study, do research and ask tough questions).

Unfortunately, some teachers these days use their classrooms to teach us their own personal and political views. So, topics like catastrophic global warming are freely taught.

Some teachers have even forced their students to watch pro-global warming documentaries or get a bad grade!

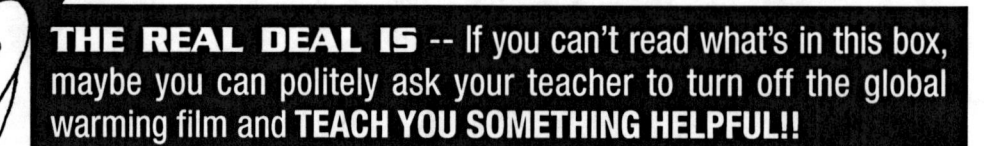

THE REAL DEAL IS -- If you can't read what's in this box, maybe you can politely ask your teacher to turn off the global warming film and **TEACH YOU SOMETHING HELPFUL!!**

POLITICIANS

Another group that rings the global warming alarm bell is politicians.

Okay, not all politicians. While some might actually believe global warming stories there are others who use global warming to become more popular with the people who voted for them. If the people believe in it, by golly so will the politician! But there's a scarier reason some politicians promote global warming. – **A much, much scarier reason!**

Huh?!

Some politicians use the global warming issue to grow bigger government and unfortunately bigger government means bigger control over what we can and cannot do in our personal lives!

In fact, several politicians have already started to create expensive new government requirements and special global warming fix-it programs all over the world. And guess who's going to have to pay for this?

More government control?! Forget global warming THAT'S scary!

You and me

Us!!

You, me, your mom, your dad, your sister, your … Well you get the picture. We'll all have to pay for extremely costly global warming remedies to fight against man-made global warming even though man-made global warming isn't even a proven fact!

THE REAL DEAL IS -- Several politicians are already in the process of concocting creative ways to make more money for government because of global warming.

BILLIONS OF REASONS TO PROMOTE GLOBAL WARMING

THE REAL DEAL IS, there are billions of reasons for some people to promote global warming catastrophe predictions that can be explained in three simple words. Ready? Here goes.

BILLIONS OF DOLLARS!

THE REAL DEAL IS -- Lots of people's wallets are benefiting from the whole global warming movement.

Let's check it out!

Some politicians have been able to build very lucrative careers off the issue while some alarmist scientists are cashing in on global warming, too.

THE REAL DEAL IS, it's not easy for most scientists and researchers to make enough money to keep their work going so scientists who can connect whatever research they're doing to global warming often get money for their work that may have been super hard to get before.

Scientist #1

Question:
"I want to study how high the 2 ½ toed tree frog can jump."

Answer:
"Sorry, go away."

Scientist #2

Question:
"I want to study how global warming affects how high the 2 ½ toed tree frog can jump."

Answer:
"Wonderful! Here's five million dollars!"

THE REAL DEAL IS -- If your money and job are dependent on the problem continuing you are less likely to say there is no problem. It leads to keeping the problem existing rather than getting rid of it!

So where do these billions of dollars come from?

You and me

Us again! You, me, your dad, your mom, your … Again, you get the picture. Alot of this money to "fix" global warming will come from us paying more taxes.

TAX - A tax is not a voluntary monetary payment but an enforced contribution, imposed by government.

Right now we're kids without jobs so we don't have to worry about being over taxed. But your parents do, and the more money they are taxed, the less money they have to buy us fun stuff.

And that is totally not cool!

"Carbon offset", just what I always wanted.

CHAPTER 8

X-TREMIE GREENIE MEANIES!!

DOWN WITH PEOPLE!

WE HEAR…

We're Green

We care!

You know how good it feels when everything in your room is clean and tidy? It's a better place to hang out, right?

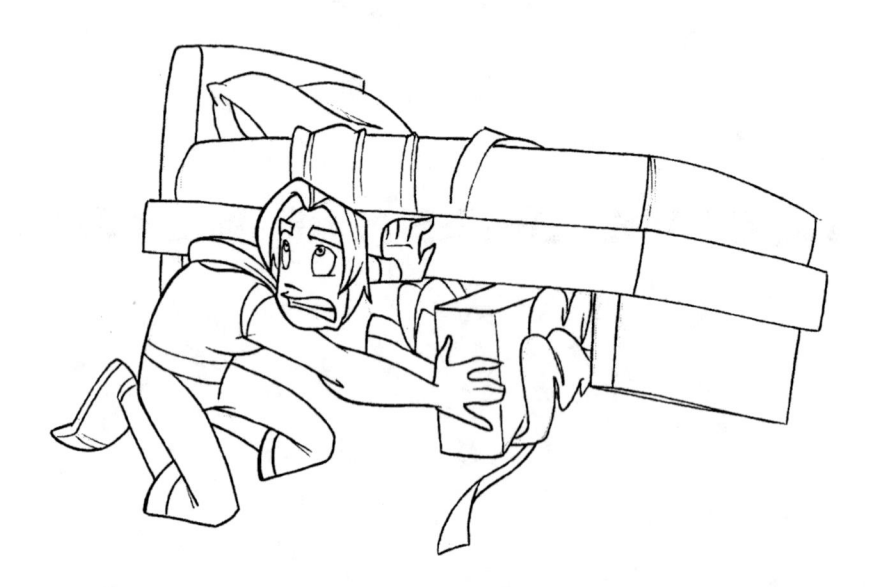

It's the same way with earth. Earth may be a little bit bigger than your room (okay a lot bigger than your room), but when earth is clean and tidy it becomes a better place to hang out, too. Luckily, there are plenty of environmental groups you can join to help keep earth nice.

BUT BEWARE!!

Not all environmental groups are the same. **THE REAL DEAL IS,** while SOME environmental groups are cool, educational and lots of fun, OTHER environmental groups are total **X-tremie Greenie Meanies!**

X-tremie Greenie Meanies are powerful environmental activist groups. And when it comes to planet earth, they've pretty much been the boss of all of us!

What's X-treamie Greenie Meenies?

EXTREME - Going to great or exaggerated lengths: Radical

ACTIVISTS - Individual who are extensively and vigorously involved in political activity, either within or outside the governmental system; militant reformers

---

!!POP QUIZ!!

Question: Who creates a problem that wasn't a problem in the first place then creates the solution to the problem that wasn't a problem in the first place that will cost us a ton of money to fix, even though the problem wasn't a problem in the first place?

Answer: X-Tremie Greenie Meanies!

There are lots of really cool environmental groups that are committed to the care of animals, plants, earth, and the people who live on earth.

X-tremie Greenie Meanies are committed to the care of animals, plants, and earth, too, but to them **PEOPLE** are **NOT** considered an important or welcomed part of earth!

These groups say that people are a **"problem"** who overpopulate the earth, use too many of its resources and pollute it beyond repair. They believe they need to save earth from people because earth is **"fragile"**.

Who are you callin' fragile?!

Okay, rude!

Leaders of these groups have even called humans names like **"the enemy"** and **"A cancer on the face of the earth."**

Their basic goal is for earth to exist in its natural, pre-modern form, untouched by people.

But there's something even scarier about these groups. **Something much, much scarier!**

"What could be scarier?"

These groups promote the type of global warming hysteria that's giving some of us nightmares!

"That's a relief!"

Luckily, not all environmental groups are X-tremie Greenie Meanies and we don't have to let meanies be the boss of us!

THE REAL DEAL IS -- The coolest environmental groups care about the earth, but care about the well-being of people too!

DOWN WITH FREEDOM!

Luckily, X-tremie Meanies and their followers are pretty easy to spot.

X-TREMIES...

Push to end industry and available energy for our homes, cars, factories.

Fight to end our personal freedoms like what we eat, how we cook, what we drive, how we drive, where we can vacation, how we can vacation!

Oh yeah, and they also...

Sound – Kind of wacky sometimes.

Did you know recently we were told we should help save the planet by using only one sheet of toilet paper?

Of course, the celebrity who said this later claimed she was "joking" (yeah, right!). **THE REAL DEAL IS**, the whole toilet paper thing may be a joke, but how **Greenie Meanies** achieve their goals is no laughing matter. Sadly, they're downright **extreme.**

Serious?!

MEAN GREEN ENVIRONMENTAL MACHINE

Activist environmental groups are no joke. They want what they want, when they want it (kind of like your baby brother or sister at a toy store, but totally kicked up a notch).

SOME OF THE WAYS X-TREMIE GREENIE MEANIES GET THEIR WAY

Physical obstruction!

Timing device explosives!

Beating corporate executives with pick-axe handles!

Blowing up private cars of animal researchers!

Firebombs!

Plots to blow up electrical towers!

Plots to blow up dams!

Destroying millions of dollars in property!

Threatening tree cutters with injury and death!!!

X-tremies frequently claim that building something will interfere with or harm nature. And there's big time pressure to give them what they want whether their claim is proven or not. Because they cause builders to lose millions of dollars to fight court battles against them; often times the builder gives up the whole idea of building where these groups don't want them to build… like the case of oil refineries.

X-tremie Greenie Meanies have fought long and hard to keep oil refineries or other energy sources from being built in the United States even though the population has grown and the U.S. really needs it.

They have fought super hard to prevent drilling for oil in the Arctic National Wildlife Refuge (ANWR). In fact X-tremies have pretty much claimed the Alaskan area of ANWR off-limits, even though drilling there could do a lot of people a lot of good.

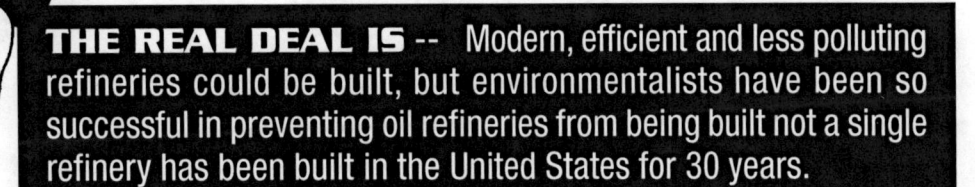

THE REAL DEAL IS -- Modern, efficient and less polluting refineries could be built, but environmentalists have been so successful in preventing oil refineries from being built not a single refinery has been built in the United States for 30 years.

THINK ABOUT WHAT DRILLING FOR OIL IN ALASKA WOULD MEAN...

More natural gas to heat homes in the winter!

Hundreds of thousands of new jobs!

Economic growth for the entire nation!

The U.S wouldn't have to remain dependent on foreign oil!

CHEAPER GAS!!

THE REAL DEAL IS -- There are 19 million acres of ANWR. 17.5 million acres are off-limits, which leaves 1.5 million acres for exploration. Only 2,000 acres is needed for drilling which leaves 99.99% of the area undisturbed if they're allowed to drill for billions of gallons of oil. But that's not acceptable to X-tremie Meanies.

Even though new oil refineries would allow us to live more efficiently, safer and cheaper, these groups fight against them. Sadly, their fight doesn't stop there. They also interfere in matters that could help us live longer and healthier lives.

People with diseases like cancer and AIDS depend on research that's sometimes done on animals. Since these groups oppose this they frequently use violence and destruction to fight against it. They've even threatened medical researchers and their families. As a result some of the research money has completely gone away and so has a lot of important research that could find cures for unknown numbers of human beings.

... AND THE WINNER OF THE MEANEST DEED BY GREENIE MEANIES IS ...

The ban on DDT!! Author Rachel Carson (the "mother of the environmental movement in the U.S"), created a world-wide panic in 1962. In her book, *(The Silent Spring)* she claimed that a pesticide called DDT was cancerous and could wipe out eagles, a species of birds. Like the global warming hysteria, DDT hysteria caught on fast. Unfortunately, mosquitoes carry a deadly disease called Malaria.

The good news is DDT is one of the most effective ways of controlling mosquito populations.

The bad news is, thanks to Rachel Carson DDT has been and remains banned in country after country, and it can not be used. As a result millions of people get malaria every year and many of them don't survive.

THE REAL DEAL IS -- DDT is a toxic poison which makes it the most powerful and long lasting pesticide in existence. It's also very cheap and spraying just a little a couple of times a year could save millions of lives!

In the time it took you to read this chapter, more than a thousand people have contracted malaria.

CHAPTER 9

THE GREENIES WHO CRIED, WOLF!!

ECO "OOPSIES!"

!!POP QUIZ!!
(Careful, this one's tricky!)

What is the following quote about?

"… The indications that our climate can soon change for the worse are too strong to be reasonably ignored."

If you said global warming, you're WRONG! *(Told you this one's tricky!)* It's about man-made global **COOLING!** But don't feel bad. When it comes to matters of our environment X-Tremies have had more than their share of wrong answers, too. In 1970's the big environmental hysteria claimed that earth was being destroyed because it was rapidly cooling. Just like today, everyone was told...

"Climatic calamity was imminent!"

"The world's scientists agree!"

But that turned out to be wrong. And this is just one of many wrong predictions made by X-tremie Greenies that frightened people unnecessarily. They've made tons more OOPSIES over the years!

Let's check it out!

Oopsy! -- In 1890's they predicted that elk were becoming extinct in Yellowstone National Park, so the park was forced to encourage elk growth. Over the next few years the numbers of elk exploded. **HOWEVER**, too many elk caused overgrazing which changed the plant life. Plants that other animals needed to eat couldn't re-grow which caused those animals to leave the park. With no aspen trees (also gone) to make dams, beavers also disappeared. Without dams, the meadows dried hard in summer and even more animals vanished!

Oopsy! -- They predicted that the earth could not sustain more than one to two billion people or we'd all starve to death. **HOWEVER**, we currently have approximately 6 billion people living on earth and lots of us are nice and fat!

Oopsy! -- There were predictions that oil rigs in the oceans would destroy fish populations. **HOWEVER**, even rusted and abandoned rigs in the Gulf of Mexico have spawned lush marine habitats that are now home to rare corals and 10,000 to 30,000 fish each!

Oopsy! -- They predicted that a damn in Tennessee was being built on the home of the endangered snail darter, so X-tremies fought against the dam being built. **HOWEVER**, it turned out the snail darter wasn't even endangered!

Oopsy! -- During the 1970s they predicted that all oil would disappear in just 31 years. **HOWEVER** we know now there's more than enough oil available!

Oopsy! -- They predicted that recycling would be less wasteful. **HOWEVER**, the mandatory recycling programs costs us more to recycle a material than to dispose of it. And instead of helping to solve the pollution problem, it adds to pollution in other ways!

Oopsy! -- They predicted that caribou would be wiped out by the Alaskan pipeline. **HOWEVER**, the caribou population actually tripled because of the heat and other environmental aspects of the pipeline. In fact there's no evidence that over thirty years of drilling in Alaska has affected the wildlife at all!

With such a long track record of scaring us, putting people last, trying to take earth back to a time when life was more difficult, and making so many wrong predictions...Why should we believe what they're say about global warming?

"I've seen a heap of trouble in my life, and most of it never came to pass."
-- *Mark Twain*

CHAPTER 10

WHAT ABOUT THE POLAR BEARS?!

BEARLY HONEST

WE HEAR…

Global Warming

Means

No More Polar Bears!!

For all of you, who are worried, sad or freaked out in general about the future of polar bears because of global warming…

CHILL-AX!

News, films, politicians and movies may tell us that polar bears are in great danger, but several actual polar bear specialists say, "Not so much!"

THE REAL DEAL IS -- They tell us a much more comforting message, that polar bears don't need us to save them from immediate doom, or for that matter, distant doom. Seriously! You don't have to worry. It's been warmer in the past and they've done fine!

Yet, we hear that global warming will cause polar bears to meet a terrible fate.

Drowning!

Extinction!

EXTINCTION - a coming to an end or dying out

But is this another **eco-Oopsy;** simply trying to get us to buy into the global warming message by using adorable polar bears?

Let's check it out!

In 2007 a photo like this one was printed of two bears
floating farther and farther out to sea. Maybe you saw it.

The headline read --

"GLOBAL WARMING SEES POLAR BEARS STRANDED ON MELTING ICE".

The first sentence of the article said --

"They cling precariously to the top of what is left of the ice floe,
their fragile grip the perfect symbol of the tragedy of global warming."

But **THE REAL DEAL IS**, this **WASN'T** a photo of stranded polar bears at all!

Huh?!

It was really a photo of a mother and her cub (taken three years earlier), **playing** on an ice sculpture created by waves. That's right!

THEY WERE PLAYING !

Playing, just like you and me when we skateboard, or speed uphill on a dirt bike. But since polar bears don't have cool stuff like skateboards and dirt bikes, they like to hang out on chunks of ice.

Speech bubble: Do you mind? I'm trying to have fun here!

Also guess what month the photo was taken?

AUGUST!

...Summer, when ice melts every year regardless of any "global warming". Yet, the media presented this photo and story to make us all feel sad about suffering polar bears. But it's a story that never happened. **THE REAL DEAL IS,** this photo had nothing to do with global warming.

Speech bubble: Okay, rude!

"This is a perfect picture for climate change…

you have the impression they are in the middle of the ocean

and they are going to die…

But they were not that far from the coast,

and it was possible for them to swim…

They are still alive and having fun."

- Spokesperson for Environmental Canada

THE REAL DEAL IS -- Not one animal extinction can be blamed on climate change!

SOME MORE HELPFUL POLAR BEAR FACTS:

- Polar bears don't use most of the ice cap because they like near shore ice better!

- Polar bears are adaptable to use land, which they do all summer long, every year!

- Even when their favorite food like ice seal occasionally declines, data indicates that polar bears adapt and use different food sources, including food sources that may be expanding!

THE REAL DEAL IS -- About 60 % of the arctic ice pack melts every summer. This is an area greater than the United States!

BEARLY TRUTHFUL

Because of global warming we're led to believe that polar bears are threatened to become endangered within 45 years.

Let's check it out!

Over the past 5,000 years the summer temperatures were warmer than now. If today's warming is pushing sea ice to shrink, then that must've also happened in the past 5,000 years (probably more so, since it was warmer for much longer in the past)! But today's existence of polar bears proves that they didn't disappear as a result of warming in the past! Polar bears have survived for thousands of years, including both colder and warmer periods.

THE REAL DEAL IS -- Arctic air temperatures were as high, or higher than at present in the 1930s and polar bears survived. They even survived the massive melting of the glaciers 10,000 years ago!

"There may be threats to the future survival of the polar bear, but global warming is not primary among them."

- The National Center for Policy Analysis

THE REAL DEAL IS -- Artic ice melts and freezes much like the falling of leaves. Polar bears have always managed to exist through all earth temperature phases.

LOTS AND LOTS OF POLAR BEARS!

There's more good news about polar bears. Polar bear specialists say the bears are currently at historic high population levels (in all but 1 or 2 regions, where they are hunted). **THE REAL DEAL IS**, there is no evidence that sea ice loss itself will cause a decline in polar bear habitat or numbers.

THE REAL DEAL IS -- Animal populations fluctuate a great deal, all the time!

SPECIALISTS ALSO SAY...

- Polar bears are abundant and their population in Alaska is healthy in size and distribution.

- The polar bear continues to occupy its entire historical range.

  And last but not least…

- Polar bear population in Churchill Alaska (the "undisputed polar capitol of the world") outgrew the food supply!

THE REAL DEAL IS -- The growth of the polar bear population in Alaska has coincided with the emergence of the oil and gas industry across the North Slope, even during a trend of warming temperatures.

STILL WORRIED?

Okay, here's something that's sure to totally make you feel better when you see heart-wrenching photos of polar bears floating in the ocean on a chunk of ice...

POLAR BEARS CAN SWIM OVER 60 MILES!

THE REAL DEAL IS, polar bears are known to be among earth's strongest swimmers. They hang out on glacier ice all the time.

In fact, they like to travel and play on them.

So, if you're worried, don't. Rest assured, animals typically know their capabilities, which means they probably know how far they can go out into the ocean and swim back safely.

Think about it...

We've all seen lots of scary images of flooding cities, destructive storms and drowning polar bears. But how fair is it to show us these images if they're not entirely **THE REAL DEAL?**

CHAPTER 11

OKAY, SO HOW DO I TAKE CARE OF THE EARTH?!

GOOD STEWARDSHIP

THE REAL DEAL IS, there are many positive ways to be eco-cool and care for and about the earth. If you're wondering how, just **CHECK IT OUT!**

REMEMBER, Catastrophic global warming is still wildly unproven and so are its "solutions". **THE REAL DEAL IS**, there have been tons of other eco-oopsies since the environmental movement started (and some have had some pretty sad results).

REMEMBER, you can care a great deal about the earth without following the latest environmental solutions. But if you choose to recycle, become a vegan, drive a corn-powered car, whatever you'd like, go for it! But also remember these are your own personal choices (and it's unlikely they are saving the earth) so don't force them on everyone else. **THE REAL DEAL IS**, that is so, X-Tremie Meanie!

REMEMBER, if someone calls you names or treats you badly because you don't believe what they believe, take joy! **THE REAL DEAL IS**, the world's greatest leaders are called leaders, not followers! You may become one of them one day!

REMEMBER to enjoy earth. It's awesome and it's our home! So don't feel bad or guilty about our use of it. **THE REAL DEAL IS**, humans aren't really the dastardly earth destroyers X-Tremie Meanies present us as!

REMEMBER, we should always be concerned about our environment and earth and by all means wisely use its natural resources. You wouldn't trash your house or your school, treat earth the same way. **THE REAL DEAL IS**, we have been called to be good stewards over it.

STEWARDSHIP - Responsibility for taking good care of resources entrusted to one.

AND LASTLY... *Pick up trash on the ground. PaPa*

REMEMBER, if you choose to join an environmental group, check them out first!

Make sure the group's practices are based on logic and facts, **NOT** emotions and fear!

Make sure they're not anti-human, anti-industry, they don't force or bully people into doing what they want.

Find out if the solutions they propose don't hurt the economy of people and the country, and they actually work without bad consequences to humans or the earth in the future.

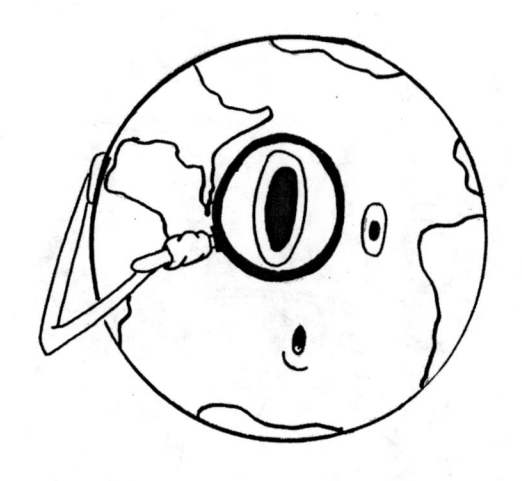

CHAPTER 12

CHECK IT OUT!

MORE REAL DEAL!

Want more cool information on global warming?

COOL PEOPLE

TIMOTHY BALL
Chairman and Chair of the Scientific Advisory

WALTER E. WILLIAMS
Phd, Economics

PAUL DRIESSEN
Author, "Eco-Imperialism: Green Power, Black Death"
Senior Fellow, Congress of Racial Equality (CORE)

JOHN CHRISTY
Professor and Director
Earth System Science Center, NSSTC
University of Alabama

A COOL MOVIE...

"THE GREAT GLOBAL WARMING SWINDEL"
Documentary (UK)

AND COOL BOOKS...
Recommended for Teens and Adults

ROY INNIS
Author, *"Energy Keepers, Energy Killers"*
Chairman, Congress of Racial Equality (CORE)

CHRISTOPHER C. HORNER
Author,
"The Politically Incorrect Guide to Global Warming"

PATRICK MICHAELS
Author
"Meltdown"

JOHN BERLAU
Author, *"Eco-Freaks"*

COOL WEBSITES

THE HEARTLAND INSTITUTE
"Reasoned thinking comes from cooler heads"
www.globalwarmingheartland.org

THE COOLER HEADS COALITION
"Reasoned thinking comes from cooler heads"
www.globalwarming.org

INTERFAITH STEWARDSHIP ALLIANCE
"Bridging humanity and the environment through faith and reason"
www.stewards.net

ABOUT THE AUTHOR

Whether she's writing and producing acclaimed primetime television shows for adults or Emmy nominated and Image Award winning children's programs, Al Sonja L. Schmidt's ability to bring stories to life is undeniable. As a concerned mother she became motivated help use her experience to ease children's growing fears about what they're being told about global warming. She plans to continue to "deal" with hot topics that impact today's youth with the *Deb & Seby* book series.

Schmidt was born and raised in South Central Los Angeles. She now resides in a scenic area in the Los Angeles National Forest with her husband and two golden retrievers, Waylon and Indy.